Snowmobiles

By Muriel L. Dubois

Consultant:
Greg Creamer
World Snowmobile Association

CAPSTONE
HIGH-INTEREST
BOOKS

an imprint of Capstone Press
Mankato, Minnesota

Capstone High-Interest Books are published by Capstone Press
151 Good Counsel Drive, P.O. Box 669, Mankato, Minnesota 56002
http://www.capstone-press.com

Library of Congress Cataloging-in-Publication Data
Dubois, Muriel L.
Snowmobiles/by Muriel L. Dubois.
    p. cm.—(Wild rides)
    Includes bibliographical references (p. 31) and index.
    ISBN 0-7368-0932-5
    1. Snowmobiles—Juvenile literature. 2. Snowmobiling—Juvenile
literature. [1. Snowmobiles. 2. Snowmobiling.] I. Title. II. Series.
TL234.2 .D83 2002
629.22'042—dc21   2001000215

Summary: Describes these winter vehicles, their history, parts, and competitions.

Editorial Credits
Matt Doeden, editor; Karen Risch, product planning editor; Kia Bielke,
    cover and interior designer; Katy Kudela, photo researcher

Photo Credits
ALLSPORT PHOTOGRAPHY, cover, 10 (bottom), 15, 16, 21, 22, 26, 28
Arctic Cat, 4 (top), 8, 14, 18
Carl Eliason Family, 12
Richard Hamilton Smith, 10 (top)
Unicorn Stock Photos/Andre Jenny, 4 (bottom), 6–7, 24

1 2 3 4 5 6 07 06 05 04 03 02

Table of Contents

Chapter One: Snowmobiles 5

Chapter Two: Early Models of Snowmobiles............ 11

Chapter Three: Designing a Snowmobile 17

Chapter Four: Snowmobiles in Competition.......... 23

Words to Know 30

To Learn More.................................. 31

Useful Addresses 31

Internet Sites..................................... 32

Index 32

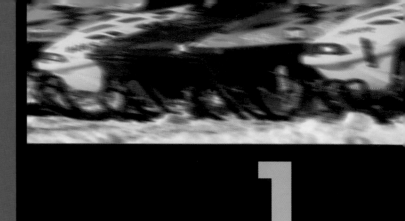

Learn about:

- **Snowmobile manufacturers**

- **Cost of snowmobiles**

- **Sponsors**

CHAPTER **1**

Snowmobiles

Fourteen snowmobiles form two rows behind
the starting line. The riders lean forward over
their snowmobiles. A flagman waves a green flag
to begin the race.

The roar of the snowmobiles' engines fills the
air. The riders approach the first turn. They lean
to one side of their snowmobiles. Their body
weight helps the snowmobiles turn quickly.

The riders then ride over a series of bumps
and jumps. The snowmobiles sail over some of
the large jumps. The riders hold on tightly as
they land.

One rider does not hold on tightly enough.
He falls off his snowmobile as it crashes into the
edge of the course. But the rider quickly gets
back on and returns to the race. He knows that
he has 15 more laps to catch the other riders.

About Snowmobiles

Snowmobiles are small vehicles designed to travel on snow and ice. Snowmobile riders often call these vehicles "sleds." A sled does not have wheels. Instead, it runs on a track. This long belt of rubber runs along the bottom of the sled. The track gives the sled good traction. This force prevents the sled from slipping and sliding.

Snowmobiles are popular across the northern United States and Canada. These areas usually are covered in snow and ice during winter.

People ride snowmobiles in open fields and along trails. Some people race snowmobiles. But most people ride them for enjoyment.

Four companies build almost all of the world's snowmobiles. Polaris and Arctic Cat snowmobiles are made in Minnesota. Ski-Doo snowmobiles are made in Quebec, Canada. Yamaha snowmobiles are made in Japan. Snowmobile riders call these four companies the "big four."

Snowmobile races are common in areas that often have snow cover.

Arctic Cat sleds are among the most popular snowmobiles.

Types of Sleds

Most people buy snowmobiles from one of the big four companies. These sleds cost around $5,000. But these snowmobiles usually are not built for racing.

Some manufacturers build high-performance stock sleds. These snowmobiles are made both for pleasure riding and for racing. They can cost as much as $10,000.

Professional snowmobile racers also may buy specially made racing sleds called "mod" or "open" sleds. These sleds may cost as much as $35,000. Racers often modify their sleds. They make changes to lighten the body or to improve engine power.

Racing sleds are expensive to maintain. Racing teams may spend $100,000 or more each year to keep a sled in top condition. Sponsors help pay these costs. These companies give racing teams money in exchange for advertising. For example, a gasoline company may sponsor a racing team. In return, the racing team puts the gasoline company's logo on the side of the snowmobile.

Learn about:

■ **Virgil White**

■ **Motor toboggans**

■ **Early races**

CHAPTER 2

Early Models of Snowmobiles

Motorized winter vehicles first appeared in the late 1800s and early 1900s. People needed vehicles that could safely travel over snow and ice. The first winter vehicles were based on cars and tractors. People used them for jobs such as hauling logs out of the woods.

The First Winter Vehicles

In 1923, inventor Virgil White replaced the front wheels of a Model T Ford with skis. He called the vehicle a snowmobile. White sold kits that allowed people to modify their cars for winter.

Other builders began with tractors. They added tracks to the wheels. The tracks prevented the vehicles from becoming stuck in the snow.

Carl Eliason built a new type of winter vehicle in 1924. He combined bicycle parts with skis and a motor to build the motor toboggan. These vehicles became popular during the 1930s. Hunters and animal trappers used motor toboggans during winter. During World War II (1939–1945), the U.S. military bought 150 motor toboggans.

Carl Eliason invented the motor toboggan in 1924.

True Snowmobiles

Inventors first built modern snowmobiles in the 1950s. These sleds had skis, tracks, and engines in the back. Two of these inventors were David Johnson and Edgar Hetteen. Johnson and Hetteen started the Polaris company. Hetteen later left Polaris. He started a new company called Polar Industries. This company later changed its name to Arctic Cat.

The first snowmobile Hetteen built at Polar Industries was the Polar 500. This was mainly a work vehicle. He later built the Arctic Cat 100 for pleasure riding.

Snowmobiles became more popular during the 1960s. Manufacturers designed quieter, more efficient engines. Most people rode these new snowmobiles for fun. Postal workers sometimes used snowmobiles to deliver mail. Rescue workers used them to reach people trapped in snow.

Manufacturers continued to improve snowmobile designs. They added headlights for night riding. Windshields protected riders' faces from snow and wind. Shock absorbers provided smoother rides.

People today still enjoy riding snowmobiles through open fields and woodlands.

Snowmobile Racing

The first organized snowmobile races were held in northern Minnesota in the mid-1960s. Riders took part in cross-country races across open fields and woodlands.

Racing grew in popularity during the early 1970s. Some riders modified their sleds for racing. Organizers built courses for snowmobile races inside arenas. People gathered to watch the riders race around these courses.

In the mid-1970s, fuel became very expensive. Fewer people wanted to take part in snowmobile races. The sport became less popular. But fuel became less expensive in the early 1980s. Snowmobile racing became popular again. Today, it remains a popular sport across the northern United States and Canada.

Snowmobile racing is popular across the northern United States and Canada.

Learn about:

- **Aerodynamics**

- **Engine sizes**

- **Safety features**

CHAPTER 3

Designing a Snowmobile

Manufacturers build snowmobiles for different purposes. Most snowmobiles are designed for pleasure riding. Some sleds are work vehicles. Others are built for racing. But all snowmobiles have the same basic parts.

Body Design

The main body of a snowmobile is called the chassis or the frame. All of the other parts connect to the chassis. The chassis usually is made of a strong, lightweight metal such as aluminum.

Manufacturers design snowmobile bodies to reduce air resistance. These designs are aerodynamic. Sleds with aerodynamic body designs can reach the highest speeds.

Designers build sleds with rounded front ends. They avoid flat surfaces at the front of the sleds. Flat surfaces create more air resistance than rounded edges.

Engines and Speed

Snowmobile engines are measured in cubic centimeters (cc). Engines may be as small as

Skis help riders turn their snowmobiles.

100cc. Most standard engines are between 400cc and 600cc. Most racing snowmobile engines are around 800cc. But some are as large as 1,000cc.

Engine size determines a snowmobile's top speed and power. A 400cc engine can reach speeds of about 70 miles (113 kilometers) per hour. A 1,000cc engine can reach speeds of more than 100 miles (160 kilometers) per hour.

Riders control their speed with the throttle. This device is connected to the handlebars. Riders press a trigger to speed up. They let go of the trigger to slow down.

Skis

A pair of skis connects to the front of the chassis. The skis allow riders to steer their sleds. Riders use the handlebars to turn the skis.

Skis are made of a smooth, durable material. Most sleds have hard plastic skis. Some sleds have metal skis. Steel is the most common metal used in skis. A sharp strip of metal runs down the middle of each ski. The strip acts as a blade. It cuts into the top layer of snow or ice to improve control.

Tracks

A set of wheels in the back of a snowmobile turns the track. The track uses the engine's power to move the sled. Snowmobile tracks include a series of bumps and grooves. This pattern provides traction. Snowmobile riders sometimes add metal studs and picks to their tracks. These items give snowmobiles even greater traction.

Riders choose their snowmobile's tracks based on the kind of riding they do. Tracks on racing sleds may have small bumps and grooves to increase speed. People who ride in mountainous areas may have tracks with larger bumps and grooves to increase traction in deep snow.

Safety Features

Snowmobile riders are concerned with safety. Sleds today are much safer than sleds of the past. Manufacturers now include many safety features on their sleds.

The windshield is one basic safety feature. This clear screen on the front of the sled protects riders' faces from cold and wind.

Snowmobiles also include headlights and reflectors. Many snowmobile riders travel alongside roads. Headlights and reflectors make these snowmobiles visible to drivers of passing cars.

Most riders use tether cords. A rider hooks one end of the cord around one arm. The other end is connected to the ignition. The cord shuts off the ignition if the rider falls off the sled. The sled then stops. A snowmobile would keep running without a tether cord.

Headlights make snowmobiles visible to drivers of passing cars.

Learn about:

■ **International Snowmobile Racing**

■ **Snocross series**

■ **Drag races**

CHAPTER 4

Snowmobiles in Competition

Men and women of many ages and abilities can compete in snowmobile races. Children take part in races based on age. Other racers can take part in races based on the size of their snowmobiles' engines. Professional racers also have their own races. These racers earn their living from snowmobile racing.

Several groups oversee the rules and guidelines for snowmobile races. One such organization is called International Snowmobile Racing (ISR). ISR makes sure snowmobile races are safe and fair for all riders.

Cross-Country Racing

Cross-country races take place across long stretches of open fields and woodlands. Some cross-country races go through mountainous areas. Race officials mark cross-country courses with barrels or flags. These markings show riders where to go. Race officials also may give riders maps of the course.

Snocross is one of the most popular forms of snowmobile racing.

24

As many as 100 riders may take part in cross-country races. The races may be as long as 1,000 miles (1,600 kilometers). Cross-country races may take several days to complete.

Snocross Racing

One popular form of snowmobile racing is Snocross. Snocross races are based on motocross races. Motocross riders race small motorcycles over winding dirt courses with bumps and jumps. Snocross racers race snowmobiles over similar courses made of snow and ice.

Professional snowmobile riders compete in the WSA Snocross Worldwide Championship Series. This group of races takes place from early December to mid-March. Riders receive points in each race depending on their finish. The rider with the best score at the end of the series is the series champion.

Top Snocross riders also may compete at the Winter X Games. The ESPN TV network hosts these games each year. Athletes in extreme sports such as snowboarding and Snocross take part in the Winter X Games.

Ice oval tracks include two straightaways and two long turns.

Other Races

Ice-oval races take place on icy oval tracks. The tracks include two straightaways and two long turns. The turns are sloped to prevent riders from skidding off the track.

Le Mans races also take place on snow or ice tracks. Le Mans tracks include one long straightaway with curves at each end. The other side of the track includes many curves, bumps, and jumps.

Drag races are held on long, straight tracks. Each drag race is called a heat. Four riders take part in each heat. The top two finishers advance to the next heat. The final heat includes the four best riders of the event.

Hillclimb races take place on steep, snow-covered hills or mountains. Riders race one at a time up the course. The rider with the fastest time wins the event. Hillcross is a new kind of hillclimb race. Six Hillcross racers climb a slope at the same time. The first one to the top wins the race.

Enduro races are held on long oval tracks. Enduro is short for "endurance." These races test a rider's ability to race for long periods of time. Enduro races may be as many as 200 laps long.

Blair Morgan

Blair Morgan is one of the most famous snowmobile racers in the world. Morgan was born in Prince Albert, Saskatchewan, Canada, on October 9, 1975. He races both snowmobiles and motocross cycles. Morgan is famous for the aerial stunts he performs during competitions. These stunts in the air earned him the nickname "Superman."

Morgan is the only person ever to win the Pro Snocross Triple Crown. Until the 1999–2000 season, Pro Snocross racing had three engine classes. Morgan won all three classes in the 1997–98 season. He won all three again in the 1998–99 season. *Snow Week Magazine* named him Racer of the Year in 1998 and 1999.

Words to Know

aerial (AIR-ee-uhl)—a stunt performed in the air

aerodynamic (air-oh-dye-NAM-mik)—designed to reduce air resistance

chassis (CHASS-ee)—the frame on which the body of a vehicle is built

modify (MOD-uh-fye)—to change; people modify a vehicle or engine in order to make it faster or more powerful.

tether (TETH-ur)—a rope that attaches a rider to a snowmobile's ignition; the tether automatically shuts off a snowmobile if the rider falls off.

throttle (THROT-uhl)—a grip or lever that controls how much fuel and air flow into an engine; a snowmobile rider presses the throttle to speed up.

traction (TRAK-shuhn)—the grip of a snowmobile's tracks on the ground

To Learn More

Armentrout, Patricia. *On Ice and Snow.*
Extreme Machines. Vero Beach, Fla.: Rourke
Press, 1998.

Mara, William P. *Snowmobile Racing.*
MotorSports. Mankato, Minn.: Capstone
Books, 1999.

Useful Addresses

Canadian Snowcross Racing Association
P.O. Box 51
Keswick, ON L4P 3E1
Canada

International Snowmobile Hall of Fame
6035 Highway 70 East
St. Germain, WI 54558

World Snowmobile Association
7351 Kirkwood Lane, #138
Maple Grove, MN 55369

Internet Sites

International Snowmobile Hall of Fame

http://www.snowmobilehalloffame.com

SnowmobileNews.com

http://snowmobilenews.rivals.com

World Snowmobile Association

http://www.wsaracing.com

Index

chassis, 17, 19
cross-country races, 14, 24–25

drag races, 27

Eliason, Carl, 12
enduro races, 27

Hetteen, Edgar, 13
hillclimb race, 27
Hillcross, 27

ice-oval races, 27
International Snowmobile
    Racing (ISR), 23

Johnson, David, 13

Le Mans races, 27

Model T Ford, 11

safety, 20–21
Snocross, 25, 29

tether cord, 21
throttle, 19

White, Virgil, 11
Winter X Games, 25